Courageous Love

Dedicated to my husband Curtis—

Thank you for showing me the
love of Jesus every day and encouraging
me to walk in His ways.
I love you always.

Courageous Love

A BIBLE STUDY ON HOLINESS FOR WOMEN

by Stacy Mitch

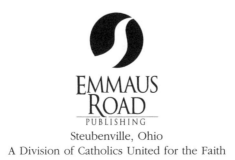

EMMAUS ROAD PUBLISHING
Steubenville, Ohio
A Division of Catholics United for the Faith

Emmaus Road Publishing
827 North Fourth Street
Steubenville, Ohio 43952

© 1999 by Emmaus Road Publishing
All rights reserved. Published 1999
Printed in the United States of America
18 17 16 15 14   10 11 12 13 14

Library of Congress Control Number: 99-90086
ISBN 0-9663223-3-9

Cover art
Orazio Gentileschi, *Annunciation* (detail)

Cover design and layout by
Beth Hart

Nihil obstat: Rev. James M. Dunfee, S.T.L.
Imprimatur. ✠ Gilbert I. Sheldon, D.D., D.Min.
Bishop of Steubenville
January 21, 1999

CONTENTS

ABBREVIATIONS

Old Testament
Gen./Genesis
Ex./Exodus
Lev./Leviticus
Num./Numbers
Deut./Deuteronomy
Josh./Joshua
Judg./Judges
Ruth/Ruth
1 Sam./1 Samuel
2 Sam./2 Samuel
1 Kings/1 Kings
2 Kings/2 Kings
1 Chron./1 Chronicles
2 Chron./2 Chronicles
Ezra/Ezra
Neh./Nehemiah
Tob./Tobit
Jud./Judith
Esther/Esther
Job/Job
Ps./Psalms
Prov./Proverbs
Eccles./Ecclesiastes
Song/Song of Solomon
Wis./Wisdom
Sir./Sirach (Ecclesiasticus)
Is./Isaiah
Jer./Jeremiah
Lam./Lamentations

Bar./Baruch
Ezek./Ezekiel
Dan./Daniel
Hos./Hosea
Joel/Joel
Amos/Amos
Obad./Obadiah
Jon./Jonah
Mic./Micah
Nahum/Nahum
Hab./Habakkuk
Zeph./Zephaniah
Hag./Haggai
Zech./Zechariah
Mal./Malachi
1 Mac./1 Maccabees
2 Mac./2 Maccabees

New Testament
Mt./Matthew
Mk./Mark
Lk./Luke
Jn./John
Acts/Acts of the Apostles
Rom./Romans
1 Cor./1 Corinthians
2 Cor./2 Corinthians
Gal./Galatians
Eph./Ephesians

Phil./Philippians
Col./Colossians
1 Thess./1 Thessalonians
2 Thess./2 Thessalonians
1 Tim./1 Timothy
2 Tim./2 Timothy
Tit./Titus
Philem./Philemon
Heb./Hebrews
Jas./James
1 Pet./1 Peter
2 Pet./2 Peter
1 Jn./1 John
2 Jn./2 John
3 Jn./3 John
Jude/Jude
Rev./Revelation (Apocalypse)

HOW TO USE THIS STUDY

The following Bible study is intended for women of all ages and walks of life. It can be used for personal enrichment as well as for small group Bible studies. A leader's guide is included in the back of the book to help those who are using it in a small group study setting.

The purpose of this Bible study is to help you discover and reflect upon what Holy Scripture teaches about women and our pursuit of holiness. In this study, you will examine and answer questions about various Scripture verses and contemplate your ideas about God, the Christian life, and your life. I have included introductions and some explanations along the way, as well as various quotes by saints, popes, and theologians, but the bulk of the work has been left up to you. At the end of each chapter is a suggested Bible verse to memorize.

The tools needed for this Bible study are a Bible, a copy of the *Catechism of the Catholic Church*, a pen, and a teachable heart. The Bible translation I used in writing this study is the Revised Standard Version, Catholic Edition (RSVCE). This is the translation used in the *Ignatius Bible* (San Francisco: Ignatius Press), which may be ordered by calling Benedictus Books toll-free at 1-888-316-2640.

Finally, the real work of the spiritual life is done in prayer. And so, it is essential that the active "doing" of this Bible study be wedded to a life of prayer. Ask the Holy Spirit to give you a teachable spirit, illumine your mind to the truths of God, and make you love Him and your neighbor perfectly so as to become holy.

PREFACE

Two of the most beautiful truths I ever discovered are that God loves me as His precious daughter and that He has a plan for my life—a plan to become like His Son and our Savior, Jesus Christ, which means becoming *holy*. These truths hit me like a ton of bricks, to put it bluntly. Following Jesus didn't mean living a good life and serving Him the best I could, but always coming short of the standard He set. Rather, being a Christian woman meant, through God's grace, becoming like my Savior in holiness and thus becoming the person God had created me to be from the very beginning of time. His plan for my life doesn't involve mediocrity, but holiness. No longer was personal holiness some far off, intangible thing that could never *really* be attained. Instead, it was the goal God wanted for me more than I wanted for myself, and He would give me the grace if only I would cooperate.

The following Bible study is written for those women who love God and desire to please Him. It is written for those of you who would like to know some of what Scripture teaches about holiness and how we, as women, can practically pursue the plan God has for our lives. Jesus has already met us at the Cross and has given us the Spirit to accomplish the good work He started in us (cf. Phil. 1:6). If we cooperate, we will be counted among the blessed as we worship before the throne of God and, with the angels, see Him face to face as He really is (cf. Rev. 7:9-11). As we will discover, this goal requires *courageous love*.

[B]ut as he who called you is holy, be holy yourselves in all your conduct; since it is written, "You shall be holy, for I am holy" (1 Pet. 1:15-16).

Holiness 101

*"and may the Lord make you increase and abound
in love to one another and to all men, as we do
to you, so that he may establish your hearts
unblamable in holiness before our God and Father,
at the coming of our Lord Jesus with all his saints."*
1 Thessalonians 3:12

Holiness is often thought of as an "up in the clouds" topic that we hear our priests talk about and something that we rightly associate with the saints. We might even think that holiness is something reserved for "holy people" like Pope John Paul II or Mother Teresa and maybe our parish priest, but not something for us. But the good news is that holiness is God's plan for every person He created! "Me, a saint?!" Take heart, the saints didn't see themselves as saints either. Saint Thérèse of Lisieux wrote in her autobiography, *The Story of a Soul*:

"You know, Mother, I have always wanted to become a saint. Alas! I have always noticed that when I compared myself to the saints, there is between them and me the same difference that exists between a mountain whose summit is lost in the clouds and the obscure grain of sand trampled underfoot by passers-by. Instead of becoming discouraged, I told myself: God cannot inspire unrealizable desires. I can, then, in spite of my littleness, aspire to holiness."[1]

Saint Thérèse of Lisieux

---

[1] St. Thérèse of Lisieux, *Story of a Soul*, John Clarke, O.C.D., trans., 3rd ed. (Washington: ICS Publications, 1996), 207.

This is from "the greatest saint of modern times," according to Pope Saint Pius X. You are in good company if you feel that becoming a saint—which is what becoming holy is all about—is a bit overwhelming. Fortunately, we need not rely on our own power. Only through the grace of God can we aim at holiness, and only through His grace will we actually become holy. Our Lord told Saint Paul, "My grace is sufficient for you, for my power is made perfect in weakness" (2 Cor. 12:9).

1. From childhood we are encouraged to dream about what we might one day become. What are your goals in life?

_____

_____

_____

What do you think is your mission in life?

_____

_____

_____

In what ways have you been pursuing your goals and living your mission?

_____

_____

_____

2. What do you think holiness is? Write your definition.

_____

_____

_____

3. According to Titus 2:11, Hebrews 12:14, and 1 Peter 1:16, who is called to holiness?

_____

_____

Have you ever looked at yourself in a carnival mirror? Your head looks way too big and your body looks too long and skinny. Thinking of this image helps me to understand holiness. You see, God knows exactly what our souls are supposed to "look like," with our desires properly ordered and our hearts overflowing with love for our Creator and neighbor. Yet, when we continue in our sin and disordered passions, our souls look less like the "image of God" and more like the carnival distortion.

The New Testament word for "holy" is *hagios* (Gk.) and means "set apart, sanctified." At our Baptism, we were made holy and brought into God's covenant family (1 Cor. 6:11), set apart to do the good works prepared for us beforehand (Eph. 2:10). However, we are all too well aware of the weaknesses of human nature—what is sometimes called *concupiscence* (cf. Catechism, nos. 1264, 1426). Saint Paul himself laments:

> [B]ut I see in my members another law at war with the law of my mind and making me captive to the law of sin which dwells in my members. Wretched man that I am! Who will deliver me from this body of death? Thanks be to God through Jesus Christ our Lord! (Rom. 7:23-25).

And so we try with God's grace to live up to the family standards established by Our Heavenly Father, but through concupiscence sometimes fall short of these standards. Throughout our lives, however, we will establish good habits and learn to obey all that God commands us and so become *righteous*. But holiness is an important step beyond righteousness. Holiness is when you are right before God in obeying all the "family rules": You love the Father and mother (Mary) and your brothers and sisters (neighbors) perfectly—you are "wholly" in love with God and His will. When our hearts and actions perfectly reflect God in us, our lives and souls no longer look like a carnival distortion of the "image and likeness of God," but rather reflect the beautiful person we were created to be. (Catechism, nos. 1987-2029 are a must read!)

4. Matthew 23 contains a stinging rebuke to the Pharisees, a Jewish sect in Jesus' day. According to Jesus in Matthew 23:23-28, how did the Pharisees misunderstand true holiness?

_____

_____

_____

How do Christians sometimes misunderstand perfection?

_____

_____

5. "All Christians in any state or walk of life are called to the fullness of Christian life and to the perfection of charity. All are called to holiness: 'Be perfect, as your heavenly Father is perfect'" (Catechism, no. 2013, citations omitted). Becoming like Jesus, the Holy One (Mk. 1:24), is the goal of the Christian life. Read Matthew 19:16-22.

a. What does Jesus tell the young man about the way to enter eternal life?

_____

_____

_____

b. What commandments does Jesus tell the young man to obey?

_____

_____

_____

c. What did Jesus tell the young man he had to do if he wished to be perfect?

_____

_____

_____

d. The young man was told that he would have treasures in heaven if he did what Jesus said he had to do to be perfect. What is it that the young man lacked?

_____

_____

_____

e. What was Jesus really asking of the young man? Why was this so difficult?

_____

_____

_____

f. What is Jesus asking you to do, if you wish to be perfect? What do you lack?

_____

_____

_____

6. Before we can pursue holiness in particular ways, we must first know the kind of heart we need to cultivate. According to the following verses, how do we prepare ourselves for pursuing holiness?

a. Sirach 2:1-6

b. Matthew 6:24

c. 2 Chronicles 7:14

d. Matthew 5:6

e. 1 Thessalonians 5:4-10

List some ways in which you could apply these truths practically in daily life.

_____

_____

_____

7. Our pursuit of holiness can become discouraging when we fail over and over again. "Isn't Jesus sick of me yet?" is a question we fight from asking ourselves too frequently. During these times of discouragement, when the devil is enjoying his way with us, we must remind ourselves of Jesus' love. Thankfully, He gives us life experiences and His Word to help us see the depth of His love. According to the following verses, what is the nature of God's love and how is it expressed?

a. John 3:16-17

b. Ephesians 2:4-7

c. Romans 5:6-8

d. Revelation 7:9-11

> "And I tell you, once we see ourselves so boundlessly loved, and see how the slain Lamb has given Himself on the wood of the Cross, the fire floods us with light, leaving no room for darkness. So enlightened by that venerable fire, our understanding expands and opens wide. And once we have experienced and accepted the light, we so clearly discern what is in God's will that we want to follow no other footsteps than those of Christ crucified, for we see well that there is no other way we can go. . . . We see that God wants only that we be made holy, and that to give us this holiness of grace God humbled Himself to become one with us. And this humility of His pulls our pride out by the roots. He is the rule we must all follow."[2]
>
> Saint Catherine of Siena

8. Our perfection is the will of God, and yet it seems very difficult. What do the following passages tell us are some of the common obstacles we confront on the road to holiness?

a. Matthew 19:16-22

b. 1 Peter 5:8

c. 1 John 2:15-16

---

[2] *The Letters of St. Catherine of Siena*, vol. 1, Suzanne Noffke, O.P., trans. (Binghamton, NY: Center for Medieval and Early Renaissance Studies, 1988), 155.

What are the causes of these struggles? What are some other "battles" on the path to perfection? How do we combat them?

_____

_____

_____

_____

_____

"Holiness consists in carrying out God's will with joy. Faithfulness forges saints. . . . The first step toward holiness is the will to attain it. With a will that is whole we love God, we opt for Him, we run toward Him, we reach Him, we possess Him. Often, under the pretext of humility, of confidence, of abandonment, we forget about using our will. But it all depends on these words—I want or I do not want. I have to pour out all my energy into the words 'I want.' We cannot decide to become saints without a great effort of renunciation, of resisting temptations, of combat, persecution, and of all sorts of sacrifices. It is not possible to love God except at one's own expense."[3]

Mother Teresa of Calcutta

9. "Be all that you can be . . . in the Christian life!" Go ahead and hum the slogan. Have you ever found yourself inspired by a homily or book to be all that God wants you to be and yet lacked the motivation to actually do anything about your feelings? The Christian life is full of little battles against the will. Read the Parable of the Sower in Mark 4:3-20. List the four types of soil, the response, the result, and Jesus' explanation of them with regard to the Christian life.

---

[3] Mother Teresa, *Heart of Joy*, José Luis Gonzalez-Balado, ed. (Ann Arbor: Servant Books, 1992), 92.

Soil	Response	Result	Jesus' Explanation
1.	1.	1.	1.
2.	2.	2.	2.
3.	3.	3.	3.
4.	4.	4.	4.

In what practical ways can we keep ourselves from being a seed that falls on "rocky soil?"

_____

_____

_____

"Thorny soil?"

_____

_____

_____

What would your life look like if the seed of God's Word were sown on good soil in your heart?

_____

_____

_____

10. Take some time to examine your life and your heart. Is this Bible study starting to get on your nerves because you're holding something back from God? Or are you excited about seeking holiness and surrendering your life completely to God, no matter the cost?

_____

_____

_____

11. Think about the subjects discussed in this week's lesson and prayerfully choose one or two ways you want to pursue God this week. Offer God your resolutions, concerns, fears, dreams, and love in prayer and let the fruit of that prayer be a week lived in courageous love for God.

_____

_____

_____

============= *Memory Verse* =============
"Strive for peace with all men, and for the holiness without
which no one will see the Lord."
Hebrews 12:14

The Dignity of Womanhood

"Holy women are an incarnation of the feminine ideal."
Pope John Paul II
Apostolic Letter On the Dignity
and Vocation of Women
(*Mulieris Dignitatem*, 1988), no. 27

Women today enjoy more political, economic, and social freedom than ever before. Our professional accomplishments, contributions, and struggles are increasingly recognized and appreciated.

Yet, women everywhere still ask themselves, "What does it mean to be a *woman?*" It seems that American women are in the midst of an identity crisis. Fortunately, Our Lord has provided us with divine wisdom in Holy Scripture and Sacred Tradition, and through Him our confusion will be replaced by the truth.

1. In what ways has modern feminism advanced the cause of women?

_____

_____

_____

_____

In what areas of life is the cause of women still in need of progress?

_____

_____

_____

"Here I cannot fail to express my admiration for those women of good will who have devoted their lives to defending the dignity of womanhood by fighting for their basic social, economic, and political rights, demonstrating courageous initiative at a time when this was considered extremely inappropriate, the sign of a lack of femininity, a manifestation of exhibitionism, and even sin!"[4]

Pope John Paul II

2. Do you find yourself confused as to the appropriate role of women in society, the workplace, and the home? Why or why not?

_____

_____

_____

_____

What do you think it means to be a woman?

_____

_____

_____

[4] Pope John Paul II, *Letter to Women* (June 29, 1995), no. 6.

3. What are some of the pitfalls of modern feminism?

_____

_____

_____

_____

How can we avoid them and continue to make true progress toward our God-given dignity and vocation?

_____

_____

_____

_____

The first settlers of America survived and started a society in unfriendly territory and, with very few resources, won a war against the world's greatest military power. With this foundational piece of history, American citizens hold the key to understanding who they are as a nation. So it is with women. We need to know where we came from, our *history*, in order to understand ourselves better.

4. Read Genesis 2:15-25.

a. What were Adam's duties in the garden? What was the commandment God gave to Adam? What would happen if he disobeyed?

_____

_____

_____

b. Why did God create Eve? Cite the verses. What do you think are the implications of these verses?

_____

_____

_____

c. How was she created? Why does Adam call her "woman"? How did Adam respond to the creation of the woman?

_____

_____

_____

d. Why does a man leave his father and mother and cleave to his wife?

_____

_____

_____

"The woman is another 'I' in a common humanity. From the very beginning they appear as a 'unity of the two,' and this signifies that the original solitude is overcome, the solitude in which man does not find 'a helper fit for him' (Gen. 2:20). Is it only a question here of 'helper' in activity, in 'subduing the earth' (cf. Gen. 1:28)? Certainly it is a matter of a life's companion, with whom, as a wife, the man can unite himself, becoming with her 'one flesh' and for this reason leaving 'his father and his mother'" (cf. Gen. 2:24).[5]

Pope John Paul II

---

[5] *On the Dignity and Vocation of Women*, no. 6 (emphasis omitted).

5. Read the story of the fall in Genesis 3 and answer the following questions. After each of your answers, explain how the answer is significant in understanding the fall.

a. When the serpent approached Eve, where was Adam?

_____

_____

b. How would Eve have known the commandment of God?

_____

_____

c. How did the serpent lure Eve into sin?

_____

_____

d. How did Adam come to eat of the tree of the knowledge of good and evil?

_____

_____

e. What is the order of persons that God addresses after eating the forbidden fruit? What does this suggest about the order of responsibility and its significance?

_____

_____

_____

f. How did Adam respond to God's questions? Eve?

_____

_____

g. What are the curses?

Serpent

Eve

Adam

h. Why do you think God directed the cherubim to guard the tree of life? What does this teach us about His mercy?

_____

_____

_____

_____

6. Baptism unchained us from original sin and the curse, yet we still must struggle against our inclination towards sin, concupiscence. We are free and yet sometimes we behave like slaves. How does Genesis 3 shed light on the strife between men and women, which is so obvious in our world? Reflect on the "pitfalls" you cited in response to question 3 and explain how they make sense of Genesis 3.

_____

_____

_____

_____

_____

"Consequently, even the rightful opposition of women to what is expressed in the biblical words, 'He shall rule over you' (Gen. 3:16) must not, under any condition, lead to the 'masculinization' of women. In the name of liberation from male 'domination,' women must not appropriate to themselves male characteristics contrary to their own feminine 'originality.' There is a well-founded fear that, if they take this path, women will not 'reach fulfillment,' but instead will deform and lose what constitutes their essential richness. It is indeed an enormous richness."[6]

Pope John Paul II

7. Jesus, through His words and actions, showed the people of His day that women are created in the image and likeness of God and deserve dignity as part of His favored creation. What do the following passages tell us about Jesus' treatment of women?

a. Mark 5:25-34

b. Luke 21:1-4

c. John 4:7-27

d. John 8:3-11

How were Jesus' actions in conflict with the prevalent cultural norms of His time?

_____

_____

---

[6] *On the Dignity and Vocation of Women*, no. 10.

8. According to the following passages, who was at the foot of the Cross during Jesus' Crucifixion?

a. Matthew 27:55-56

b. Mark 15:40-41

c. Luke 23:49

d. John 19:25-26

Were the apostles present?

_____

What do you think this teaches us about the character and strength of women?

_____

_____

What are the gifts of women that Jesus desired to highlight by ensuring that their bravery was recorded in all four Gospels?

_____

_____

9. Every Christian must agree with Saint Paul (1 Cor. 15:17) that the Resurrection is the cornerstone of Christianity and the most miraculous event in history! According to the following passages, who were the first witnesses of Jesus' Resurrection?

a. John 20:11-18

b. Mark 16:1-11

Why do you think Jesus chose to reveal Himself in this way?

_____

_____

Jesus treated women with the great dignity that God had given them from the moment of their creation. But do not be misled: Jesus was not a feminist in the way our culture understands it. Through Jesus we come to a fuller understanding of what God intended from the beginning. Jesus appointed men to have authority in the Church, and He called twelve men to lead, teach, and administer the sacraments. In Jesus' own family, we know that Mary submitted to the authority of Joseph. However, through a woman God chose to be born and raised. She was made the Queen of Heaven and set the supreme example for others on earth. Why? Because from creation man is the first in the order of authority and woman is the first in the order of love. While the man is the head of the family, the woman is the heart, and they are mutually dependent.[7] Man and woman were created to complement one another!

But love supersedes obedience. When we discover this truth we can praise God for the privileges of being a woman and understand that we are not second best or an afterthought in creation. We are different in a beautiful and necessary way, and if we deny our differences we deny our uniqueness and our beauty. From this vantage point we can go on to study what it means to exercise Christian virtues as a woman, with our

---

[7] Pope Pius XI, Encyclical Letter On Chaste Wedlock *Casti Connubii* (1930), no. 27.

natural inclination to love helping us attain holiness. We look to Mary as our mother, the perfect example of love and holiness. Pray for us, O Holy Mother of God, that we may be made worthy of the promises of Christ!

Memory Verse
"And Mary said, 'Behold,
I am the handmaid of the Lord;
let it be to me according to your word.'
And the angel departed from her."
Luke 1:38

Faith and the Life of Grace

*"Now faith is the assurance of things hoped for,
the conviction of things not seen."*
Hebrews 11:1

All the plans and resolutions made throughout this Bible study will fail without the grace of God. Only through faith in His power to work in our lives—through the merits of Jesus Christ and the sacramental life of grace offered to us by Mother Church—can we be made holy. We have faith that Our Heavenly Father will provide for all our needs, both physical and spiritual, and that He will remain true to His Word. He promised that He would complete the good work He began in us, and so we take Him at His Word (cf. Catechism, no. 1814).

1. Faith is the basis of our Christian belief. Answer the following questions:

How is faith acquired? Philippians 1:29	
What is faith? Hebrews 11:1	
What is faith's importance? Hebrews 11:6	

2. What are the "things hoped for" and the "things not seen" which faithful Christians believe?

> "Now the act of believing is an act of the intellect assenting to the divine truth at the command of the will, moved by the grace of God."[8]
>
> Saint Thomas Aquinas

The Church speaks of the *obedience of faith* by which we submit ourselves totally to God as He reveals Himself to us (Catechism, no. 143). Our faith involves both our *intellect* affirming the truths of God and our *will* acting on the truths to which we have assented. As my husband says, "faith [act of intellect] and faithfulness [act of will] are two sides of the same coin."

3. Hebrews 11 could be called "The Faithful Hall of Fame." Read Hebrews 11 and list the deeds that exemplified the faith of those listed.

Person(s)	Deed(s)
Abel	
Enoch	
Noah	
Abraham	

---

[8] *Summa Theologica* IIa-IIae, 2, 9.

Sarah	
Isaac	
Jacob	
Joseph	
Moses	
The People	
Rahab	
Gideon, Barak, Samson, Jephthah, David, Samuel, and the prophets	
Women and others	

4. Elsewhere in Scripture we are told of the connection between faith and faithfulness. How do the following passages explain this relationship?

a. Matthew 7:21

b. John 3:36

c. Romans 1:4-6

d. Galatians 5:6

5. The Bible is filled with stories of women who showed exemplary faith. Read the stories of these New Testament women and answer the questions about their faith.

	Mt. 15:21-28	Mk. 5:24-34	Lk. 1:26-38
What was her faith in?			
How did she show her faith?			
What was God's response to her faith?			
How was her life different because of her faith?			

6. If the Bible were being written today, what would be written about your faith?

	YOU!
What is your faith in?	
How do you show your faith?	
What is God's response to your faith?	

How is your life different because of your faith?	
Name an event in your life that has increased your faith.	

"The purpose of the sacraments is to sanctify men, to build up the Body of Christ and, finally, to give worship to God. Because they are signs they also instruct. They not only presuppose faith, but by words and objects they also nourish, strengthen, and express it. That is why they are called 'sacraments *of faith*.'"

Catechism, no. 1123

The *sacraments* of the Church give us the grace to become holy. The Holy Eucharist, "the source and summit of the Christian life,"[9] gives us the body, blood, soul, and divinity of Jesus, who becomes part of us so we can be more like Him.

7. In the "Bread of Life Discourse," Jesus tells us in His own words about the substance of the Holy Eucharist, its importance, and its necessity in our lives. Read John 6:47-63.

a. According to Jesus, what is the bread of life?

_____

_____

b. What will happen to those who eat the body and blood of Jesus?

_____

_____

---

[9] Catechism, no. 1324, quoting Vatican II's Dogmatic Constitution on the Church (*Lumen Gentium*), no. 11.

c. Why were the disciples offended at Jesus' saying?

_____

_____

d. What does Jesus mean in verses 62 and 63?

_____

_____

> "Our Savior has instituted the most august sacrament of the
> Eucharist, which contains his flesh and blood in their reality, so
> that whoever eats of it shall live forever. Therefore whoever
> turns to it frequently and devoutly so effectively builds up his
> soul's health that it is almost impossible for him to be poisoned
> by evil affection of any kind."[10]
>
> Saint Francis de Sales

8. The verses from John's Gospel, along with 1 Corinthians
11:23-32, explain the power of the Eucharist. What is required
of us to receive the body and blood of Jesus worthily? What
happens to us if we receive unworthily?

_____

_____

_____

_____

_____

---

[10] St. Francis de Sales, *Introduction to the Devout Life*, John K. Ryan trans. (Garden
City, NY: Image Books, 1972), 114.

9. How does the Eucharist help us to become holy? How does this knowledge increase your motivation to attend Mass more regularly? How will you put this sentiment into action this week?

_____

_____

_____

_____

_____

_____

_____

_____

Memory Verse

"So Jesus said to them, 'Truly, truly, I say to you,
unless you eat the flesh of the Son of man
and drink his blood, you have no life in you;
he who eats my flesh and drinks my blood
has eternal life, and I will raise
him up at the last day.'"
John 6:53-54

Love:
To Serve Is to Reign!

*"And walk in love, as Christ loved us
and gave himself up for us, a fragrant
offering and sacrifice to God."*
Ephesians 5:2

As I watched my newborn daughter, connected to a supply of oxygen and IV tubes and fighting a bacterial infection in a neonatal intensive care unit, I reflected upon the incredible love of God. Yes, it was a grace-filled moment to be sure, which taught me an important lesson I badly needed to learn. I intellectually knew that God loved her more than I ever could, and yet I was dumbfounded how it could be possible. Elizabeth did nothing to deserve my love and yet, only hours after her birth, I would have laid down my life for her in a heartbeat. I was actually amazed at how God could expand my heart to love so deeply. I came to a much deeper understanding of how God loved me—completely and without reservation. And He, the greatest lover and physician, seeing me sick in sin, laid down His life for me on the Cross.

"Charity is the theological virtue by which we love God above all things for his own sake, and our neighbor as ourselves for the love of God" (Catechism, no. 1822). And Saint Paul tells us, "So faith, hope, love abide, these three; but the greatest of these is love" (1 Cor. 13:13). Love is the greatest of all virtues because God is love (1 Jn. 4:8). And, by learning to love better and more deeply, we allow ourselves to become more like Jesus. Love makes all the difference in our pursuit of holiness.

1. We all know that God's love is beyond our complete comprehension. Yet He communicates His love to us in many ways. What do the following scriptural passages tell us about God's love for us?

a. Jeremiah 31:3

b. John 17:22-26

c. Romans 5:8

d. 1 John 3:1-2

What adjectives would you use to characterize the love of God as described in these verses?

_____

_____

What is the example of behavior God is setting for us?

_____

_____

In a typical marriage preparation program, a couple will learn that marriage is a *commitment*, a decision to love each other throughout their lives. They are cautioned that, at times, this commitment will be tested and they may not feel like loving their spouse, but they must remain steadfast in their choice to love each other.

This same principle holds true in our relationship with God. We must remember that love for God is not just an emotion but a decision that we make. Emotional love for God is a grace and a blessing, but we need to show God that we love Him in our obedience and prayer even when we do not feel like it.

2. Understanding that Jesus loves you is of paramount importance. Is it ever difficult for you to really believe this fact? Why or why not?

_____

_____

As you discover God's love for you, what is your response? How could it be different if you understood God's love more completely?

_____

_____

_____

3. Read 1 Corinthians 13.

a. List the spiritual gifts and virtues used to illustrate the preeminence of love.

_____

_____

_____

b. What are the characteristics of love? Evaluate how well you love.

_____

_____

_____

_____

_____

c. Why will the spiritual gifts pass away?

_____

_____

d. What are the childish things Saint Paul is talking about?

_____

_____

e. What have you mistaken for love?

_____

_____

f. What "childish things" are preventing you from loving fully?

_____

_____

"Love is itself the fulfillment of all our works. There is the goal; that is why we run: we run toward it, and once we reach it, in it we shall find rest."[11]

Saint Augustine

4. According to the following verses, why does our love require action?

a. Matthew 7:17-23

b. Galatians 5:6

c. James 2:20-26

[11] As quoted in Catechism, no. 1829.

"I realize that salvation depends directly upon the will. We are saved or damned according to what we love. If we love God, we shall ultimately get God: we shall be saved. If we love self in preference to God then we shall get self apart from God: we shall be damned."[12]

Frank Sheed

5. From Our Lord's example and commands in both the Old and the New Testaments, we know that we need to respond actively to His love. According to the following verses, how are we to turn our love into action?

a. Deuteronomy 10:12-13

b. Romans 13:8-10

c. 1 John 3:16

"Let us be reminded also of St. Thérèse of Lisieux who asked, 'How can I show my love, since love is manifested in actions?' She used to plant flowers: 'I will not miss any sacrifice, any gesture of sensitivity, any word. . . . Doing the smallest things out of love . . . I will always sing about it, even though roses are to be taken care of in the midst of thorns. The larger and sharper the thorns, the sweeter my song will be.' Our God needs our love, but he does not need our actions. The same God who does not need to tell us if he is hungry does not feel abashed at asking the Samaritan woman for some water to drink. He was indeed thirsty, but when he said, 'Give me a drink,' he who was the Creator was asking for love from his creature (see Jn. 4:4-30)."[13]

Mother Teresa of Calcutta

---

[12] Frank Sheed, *Theology and Sanity* (New York: Sheed & Ward, 1946), 3.
[13] *Heart of Joy*, 96.

6. Jesus is the perfect model of all the virtues but, in His mercy, He has also made one of His creatures, Mary, a perfect model of virtue. Let us look at one of the most important moments in all of history—one that teaches us how to love. Read Luke 1:35-38.

a. Mary calls herself "the handmaid of the Lord." The Greek word for handmaid is *doulē*, the term used for a female slave. What is Mary saying when she calls herself the *doulē* of the Lord? What does Mary's response to God tell us about her faith and love for Him?

_____

_____

_____

_____

b. What are some of the stumbling blocks in your life that prevent you from serving and loving God wholeheartedly as Mary did? What can you do to remove or overcome them?

_____

_____

_____

_____

c. Reflect upon "let it be done unto me according to thy word." What does this phrase mean?

_____

_____

_____

_____

d. What Eve did with her "yes" to Satan, Mary undid with her "yes" to God. What does Mary's "yes" ("let it be done") teach us about real love? About being holy?

_____

_____

_____

Think of one area of your life where you need to give God your "yes." Do it right now.

"She who at the Annunciation called herself the 'handmaid of the Lord' remained throughout her earthly life faithful to what this name expresses. In this she confirmed that she was a true 'disciple' of Christ, who strongly emphasized that his mission was one of service: the Son of Man 'came not to be served but to serve, and to give his life as a ransom for many' (Mt. 20:28). In this way Mary became the first of those who, 'serving Christ also in others, with humility and patience lead their brothers and sisters to that King whom to serve is to reign,' and she fully obtained that 'state of royal freedom' proper to Christ's disciples: to serve means to reign!"[14]

Pope John Paul II

7. We learn from Mary that the ideal woman is one who is completely open to God's will and whose heart is overflowing with a love that is ready and willing to serve. Reflect upon Matthew 20:25-28 and Pope John Paul II's statement, "to serve means to reign."

---

[14] Pope John Paul II, Encyclical Letter Mother of the Redeemer *Redemptoris Mater* (1987), no. 41.

a. What is Jesus telling us about the way to holiness?

_____

_____

_____

b. What does the Pope mean by "to serve means to reign"?

_____

_____

_____

8. How could you be a better servant in your daily life?

_____

_____

_____

Where have you fallen short and what are some of the obstacles?

_____

_____

_____

How can you overcome your obstacles and do better in the coming week? Choose one way you will serve the Lord well this week.

_____

_____

_____

_____

_____

"O my God! Will Your justice alone find souls willing to immolate themselves as victims? Does not Your *Merciful Love* need them too? On every side this love is unknown, rejected; those hearts upon whom You would lavish it turn to creatures, seeking happiness from them with their miserable affection; they do this instead of throwing themselves into Your arms and accepting Your infinite *Love*. O my God! Is Your disdained Love going to remain closed up within Your Heart? It seems to me that if You were to find souls offering themselves as victims of holocaust to Your Love, You would consume them rapidly; it seems to me, too, that You would be happy not to hold back the waves of infinite tenderness within You. If Your Justice loves to release itself, this Justice *which extends only over the earth*, how much more does Your Merciful Love desire to *set souls on fire* since Your Mercy *reaches to the heavens*. O my Jesus, let me be this happy victim; consume Your holocaust with the fire of Your Divine Love!"[15]

Saint Thérèse of Lisieux

Memory Verse

"It shall not be so among you; but whoever
would be great among you must be your servant,
and whoever would be first among you must be your slave;
even as the Son of man came not to be served but to serve,
and to give his life as a ransom for many."
Matthew 20:26-28

---

[15] *Story of a Soul*, 180-81.

Prayer:
The Way to a New Heart

*"Then you will call upon me and come
and pray to me, and I will hear you.
You will seek me and find me;
when you seek me with all your heart,
I will be found by you, says the LORD."*
Jeremiah 29:12-14

Do you remember the first time you fell in love? "Butterflies," goose bumps, and a longing to be together are a few of my fond memories of my first experiences with my future husband. I wanted to discover everything there was to know about my husband and to plan how we might serve Jesus together and build a family. We talked for hours because we were (and are) in love. All the more should this be true in our love affair with our heavenly Groom.

"Then you will call upon me and come and pray to me, and I will hear you. You will seek me and find me; when you seek me with all your heart" (Jer. 29:12-13). Meditate on these verses for a few moments. I must admit that this is one of my favorite scriptural passages because it is so encouraging. Through prayer we are given the gift and privilege of fellowship with God. We can talk with the Almighty Creator of the universe! Because prayer is an essential experience of God in which He can choose to reveal His mysteries and where we can show Him our love and devotion, we need to learn to do it better and more often. "Lord, teach us to pray" (Lk. 11:1).

1. Prayer is the heart of the Christian life. How would you evaluate your prayer life? Remember that God loves you and waits for you to seek Him.

_____

_____

_____

_____

_____

2. Because God is Our Father and knows what is best for us, He teaches us how to pray. What do the following verses command us to do? What do they say about the things God desires for us?

a. Matthew 7:7

_____

_____

b. Matthew 26:41

_____

_____

c. Ephesians 6:18

_____

_____

d. 1 Thessalonians 5:16-18

_____

_____

e. Colossians 4:2

_____

_____

How can we more faithfully obey the commands He gives us in these verses?

_____

_____

> "We must love prayer. It widens the heart to the point of making it capable of containing the gift that God makes of himself. Ask and seek, and your heart will be widened to welcome him and to keep him within itself."[16]
>
> Mother Teresa of Calcutta

3. I am convinced that if we believed in our need for and the effectiveness of prayer, we would never get off our knees! According to the following passages, what are the advantages of prayer for the believer?

a. John 15:7

b. Deuteronomy 4:29

c. Mark 11:24

d. Psalm 145:18-19

e. James 5:16

_____

[16] *Heart of Joy*, 114.

What did you learn from these passages that motivates you to pray?

_____

_____

"Since prayer places our intellect in the brilliance of God's light and exposes our will to the warmth of his heavenly love, nothing else so effectively purifies our intellect of ignorance and our will of depraved affections. . . . [B]y keeping close to our Savior in meditation and observing his words, actions, and affections we learn by his grace to speak, act, and will like him."[17]

Saint Francis de Sales

4. Jesus often taught using parables. Answer the following questions concerning a few of His parables:

	Luke 11:5-13	Luke 18:1-8	Luke 18:9-14
How are we to pray?			
What is the result of prayer?			
How can we apply this teaching?			

"Whether or not our prayer is heard depends not on the number of words, but on the fervor of our souls."[18]

Saint John Chrysostom

_____

[17] *Introduction to the Devout Life*, 81.
[18] As quoted in *Catechism*, no. 2700.

5. Jesus not only told His followers how they are to pray, but also gave them an example of prayer. We were given the Our Father as our model. Read Matthew 6:9-13. According to the Our Father, what should be included in our prayers and in what order?

_____

_____

_____

_____

How can your prayer life better reflect the pattern of prayer given to us by Jesus in the Our Father?

_____

_____

6. In seeking holiness, we want to become like Jesus. According to Mark 1:35, Mark 6:46-47, Luke 5:16, Luke 6:12, Matthew 26:36-45, and John 17, when, how, where, and for what did Jesus pray?

	Jesus' Prayer Life
When?	
How?	
Where?	
What?	

7. There are many beautiful examples of prayerful women throughout Scripture. We would do well to imitate Hannah, a model of motherhood and effective prayer. Read 1 Samuel 1:1–2:10. What did Hannah want and why? (See Ps. 127:3.)

_____

_____

How would you describe the way Hannah prayed? Taking her as an example, how should we pray?

_____

_____

_____

How was Hannah changed through her prayer? Why? Can we expect to be changed?

_____

_____

How did Hannah respond when God gave her the desires of her heart? How should we respond to God's action in our lives?

_____

_____

_____

8. After learning from the teachings and example of Jesus, what do you think your prayer life should look like? Write down your plan of action and make a commitment to God to do it.

_____

_____

_____

_____

"Prayer cannot be reduced to the spontaneous outpouring of interior impulse: in order to pray, one must have the will to pray. Nor is it enough to know what the Scriptures reveal about prayer: one must also learn how to pray. Through a living transmission (Sacred Tradition) within 'the believing and praying Church,' the Holy Spirit teaches the children of God how to pray."

Catechism, no. 2650

It is thus important to know what Sacred Tradition tells us about prayer. A reading of the Catechism's section on "Christian Prayer" is highly recommended, particularly nos. 2697-2724.

Memory Verse

"The Lord is near to all who call upon him, to all who call upon him in truth. He fulfils the desire of all who fear him, he also hears their cry, and saves them."

Psalm 145:18-19

Obedience:
The Proof of Our Love

"but whoever keeps his word, in him truly love for God is perfected.
By this we may be sure that we are in him."
1 John 2:5

It was a test of my authority. "Elizabeth, come here," I told my two-year-old and, knowing exactly what I was asking of her, she looked at me with her big blue eyes and refused to budge. My daughter offered me an opportunity to teach her obedience to authority. This simple childhood lesson will reap eternal rewards, as she learns to obey not only adult authority, but also to obey God as the supreme authority.

How well we learned obedience in childhood and humility in adulthood often determines our level of obedience to Our Heavenly Father. Jesus said, "Not every one who says to me, 'Lord, Lord,' shall enter the kingdom of heaven, but he who does the will of my Father who is in heaven" (Mt. 7:21). These words and others like them encourage us to take seriously our need to obey out of holy fear and, more perfectly, out of deep love for our just and most gracious God.

> "Let me picture and consider myself as standing in the presence of my judge on the last day, and reflect what decision in the present matter I would then wish to have made. I will choose now the rule of life that I would then wish to have observed, that on the day of judgment I may be filled with happiness and joy."[19]
> Saint Ignatius of Loyola

---

[19] St. Ignatius of Loyola, *The Spiritual Exercises of St. Ignatius*, Louis J. Puhl, S.J., trans. (Chicago: Loyola University Press, 1951), 77.

1. As children of God, we often behave as children and question why we must obey Our Heavenly Father. God knows us better than we know ourselves, and often reminds us why we must obey. According to the following verses, what are the logical reasons for our obedience to God? What do these verses teach us about God?

a. Matthew 7:21-27

_____

_____

b. 1 Corinthians 9:24-27

_____

_____

c. Ephesians 5:5-6

_____

_____

d. 1 John 2:17

_____

_____

In what practical ways does the knowledge of God's characteristics inspire you?

_____

_____

_____

_____

2. Holiness is about loving God completely and with total abandonment. According to the following verses, what does it mean to love God?

a. John 14:15

b. John 14:23-24

c. 1 John 5:3

d. John 15:14

What are the privileges of loving God?

_____

_____

_____

Describe the love you have for family members and friends, and how you treat them.

_____

_____

_____

_____

Describe your love for God, and how you treat Him.

_____

_____

_____

_____

Does your life reflect the knowledge that God is your first priority? (See Matthew 10:37-39.)

_____

_____

_____

"If, like the young man in the Gospel, we turn our backs and go away sad when the Lord tells us what we must do to be perfect, what do you want His Majesty to do? For He must give the reward in conformity with the love we have for Him. And this love, daughters, must not be fabricated in our imaginations but proved by deeds. And don't think He needs our works; He needs the determination of our wills."[20]

Saint Teresa of Avila

3. Because Jesus has called us to suffer with Him so that we might rise to eternal life, we should anticipate that the blessing and rewards for our obedience will be given in heaven. While, for the most part, we will have to wait until we enter our eternal rest for our reward, Scripture does speak of blessings in this life that come with obedience. According to the following verses, what are some of these blessings?

a. Isaiah 3:10

b. John 15:10-11

c. James 1:25

---

[20] *The Collected Works of St. Teresa of Avila*, Vol. 2 (*The Interior Castle*), Kieran Kavanaugh, O.C.D., and Otilio Rodriguez, O.C.D., trans. (Washington: ICS Publications, 1980), 308.

What blessings of obedience have you experienced in your own life and seen in the lives of others?

_____

_____

4. This life is a "spiritual boot camp." Through the grace of God in Baptism we are brought into the Family of God and, throughout the rest of our lives, we must respond to His love with our *obedient love*. What do the following verses tell us are the eternal blessings of obedience?

a. 2 Corinthians 5:10

b. 1 Peter 5:4

c. Revelation 22:12

d. Revelation 22:14

How would you describe your understanding and perspective of the last things—death, judgment, heaven, and hell?

_____

_____

_____

How would your life be different if you thought about death, judgment, heaven, and hell daily?

_____

_____

_____

5. We know that we should obey God because that is what's best for us. Yet we sometimes sin by giving in to temptations. According to the following verses, what should be our reaction to temptations?

a. 1 Corinthians 10:13

b. James 1:13-15

c. Hebrews 12:3-4

We have a responsibility to avoid the near occasions of sin, meaning those situations in which we are prone to fall into sin. What are some typical situations in which you sin?

_____

_____

How can you avoid these situations?

_____

_____

"The devil sets up another dangerous temptation: self-assurance in the thought that we will in no way return to our past faults and worldly pleasures. . . . For since the devil sees that he is dealing with a soul that can do him harm and bring profit to others, he uses all his power so that it might not rise. Thus, however many delights and pledges of love the Lord gives you, never proceed with such self-assurance that you stop fearing lest you fall again; and be on guard against the occasions of sin."[21]

Saint Teresa of Avila

---
[21] Ibid. (*The Way of Perfection*), 190.

6. Sin is doing what we know we should not do, or failing to do what we know we should do. Read Acts 5:1-11.

Who was Sapphira?

_____

How did she sin?

_____

_____

What happened to her as a result of her sin?

_____

_____

Why do you think she did what she did?

_____

_____

What was Peter's response to Sapphira?

_____

_____

What lesson can you learn from the story of Sapphira?

_____

_____

7. Sometimes we mistakenly think that our battle against sin only involves ourselves. Read Ephesians 6:10-18.

a. Against whom is our struggle?

_____

_____

b. What are the two "offensive weapons" or things that we can do to fight the devil?

_____

_____

c. How can these "weapons" be used to our advantage?

_____

_____

d. Write down two ways that you are going to "use your weapons" this week.

_____

_____

> Saint Michael the Archangel, defend us in battle. Be our protection against the malice and snares of the devil. May God rebuke him, we humbly pray, and do thou, O Prince of the Heavenly Host, through the power of God, cast into hell Satan and all the evil spirits who prowl about the world seeking the ruin of souls.

8. Think about the difficult areas of your spiritual life. What things do you seem to confess every time you go to Confession?

_____

_____

Why do you choose to sin in the way you do? Is there a "root" issue that needs to be dealt with?

_____

_____

Are you avoiding the "near occasion" of sin? How can you improve in this area?

_____

_____

Spend some time in prayer contemplating 1 Corinthians 9:26-27.

════════════ *Memory Verse* ════════════
"For this is the love of God,
that we keep his commandments.
And his commandments
are not burdensome."
1 John 5:3

Purity:
The Way to See God

"Blessed are the pure in heart, for they shall see God."
Matthew 5:8

Purity of heart is being able to say of Jesus, with the Psalmist,

Whom have I in heaven but thee? And there is nothing upon earth that I desire besides thee. My flesh and my heart may fail, but God is the strength of my heart and my portion for ever (Ps. 73:25-26).

An undivided heart is what we seek—a heart undefiled by the world and united to the Sacred Heart of Jesus.

1. The words "pure" and "purity" have many synonyms. Write down as many as you can. Use a thesaurus if you like.

_____

_____

_____

2. Using a dictionary, write the definitions for "pure" and "purity."

_____

_____

_____

3. Purity and purity of heart are extensively discussed throughout the Bible. What is the reason given for the exhortation to purity in each of the following verses?

a. 2 Corinthians 7:1

b. 2 Timothy 2:21

c. James 4:8

> "Blessed are the clean in heart, for they shall see God. A man is really clean of heart when he has no time for the things of this world but is always searching for the things of heaven, never failing to keep God before his eyes and always adoring him with a pure heart and soul."[22]
>
> Saint Francis of Assisi

4. What are the blessings that purity of heart brings according to the following passages?

a. Matthew 5:8

b. Job 8:5-6

c. 1 Timothy 4:8

d. Psalm 73:1

---

[22] *The Admonitions*, XVI, as quoted in John A. Hardon, S.J., ed., *The Treasury of Catholic Wisdom* (New York: Doubleday, 1987), 223.

5. We often read in Scripture about "seeing God." What does it means to "see God"?

_____

_____

_____

What kind of a life do you want to be able to present to Jesus when you see Him face to face?

_____

_____

_____

> "The 'pure in heart' are promised that they will see God face to face and be like him. Purity of heart is the precondition of the vision of God. Even now it enables us to see *according to* God, to accept others as 'neighbors'; it lets us perceive the human body—ours and our neighbor's—as a temple of the Holy Spirit, a manifestation of divine beauty."
>
> Catechism, no. 2519

6. If we want to be pure, we must learn how we are to become pure. According to the following verses, how are we to become pure?

a. Psalm 24:3-6

b. Psalm 119:9

c. Colossians 3:5

d. 1 John 3:2-3

"Purification of the heart demands prayer, the practice of chastity, purity of intention and of vision. Purity of heart requires the modesty which is patience, decency, and discretion. Modesty protects the intimate center of the person."

Catechism, nos. 2532-33

7. According to the Catechism, modesty is a central aspect of purity. What is modesty? Use your own words, but you may wish to refer to Catechism, nos. 2521-24.

_____

_____

8. From the beginning of creation, men have loved the feminine physique. However, because of this strong attraction to our physical beauty, we must be careful to handle ourselves properly. According to the following verses, how are women to dress? What should be the source of a woman's beauty? What behavior is appropriate for women?

a. 1 Timothy 2:9-10

_____

_____

b. 1 Peter 3:1-4

_____

_____

c. Titus 2:3-5

_____

_____

d. Proverbs 31:30

_____

_____

How do these principles apply to single women and girls?

_____

_____

_____

9. "[E]very one who looks at a woman lustfully has already committed adultery with her in his heart" (Mt. 5:28). "And he said to his disciples, 'Temptations to sin are sure to come; but woe to him by whom they come! It would be better for him if a millstone were hung round his neck and he were cast into the sea, than that he should cause one of these little ones to sin'" (Lk. 17:1-2). Have you ever thought about the effects of your modesty or lack of modesty on the men who see you?

_____

_____

10. Describe the types of attire that constitute "modest dress."

_____

_____

What types of clothing would Jesus think appropriate? What modern fashions would Mary wear? Which would she avoid?

_____

_____

_____

11. Take a few minutes to reflect upon your attitude about what you have just studied. Are you battling a poor attitude about changing your dress or behavior? Applying the ideas learned in this chapter, how can you strive toward holiness in the coming week? Remember that the devil wants to discourage us and to tell us lies all the time. He did it to Eve and he will do it to you. Be on your guard!

_____

_____

_____

Memory Verse
"Whom have I in heaven but thee?
And there is nothing upon earth that I desire besides thee.
My flesh and my heart may fail, but God is the strength
of my heart and my portion for ever."
Psalm 73:25-26

Discipline: The Practice of the Christian Life

"for God did not give us a spirit of timidity but a spirit of power and love and self-control."
2 Timothy 1:7

When I was in high school, I ran on our cross-country team. Our coach told us that we needed to run six days a week on our own during the summer months to prepare ourselves for the fall season. So, no matter how hot it got or how sick I felt, I diligently ran at least six days a week. I was disciplined and determined to be the best runner I could be with the natural gifts I was given.

It is no coincidence that Saint Paul uses the analogy of an athlete competing in a race (e.g., 2 Tim. 2:5) to describe the life of a Christian. The Christian life requires discipline because we are not simply preparing ourselves for a race, but for our heavenly home.

1. How would you describe a self-disciplined life and its benefits?

_____

_____

_____

_____

2. Scripture teaches us that our deeds, words, and minds need to be conformed to God's law. How do the following passages explain the need to reform our deeds, words, and minds, respectively?

a. Romans 7:19-25

b. James 3:2-8

c. Romans 12:1-2

3. The practical solution to our need to reform our lives is *discipline*. According to Proverbs 6:23 and 1 Peter 1:13-16, what are the benefits of a disciplined life?

_____

_____

_____

_____

"Let's face it, we humans really don't want God to love us *that* much. It's simply too demanding. Obedience is one thing, but this sort of love clearly calls for more than keeping commandments. It calls for nothing less than total self-donation. That might not be a difficult job for the three infinite Persons of the Trinity, but for creatures like us, such love is a summons to martyrdom. This invitation requires much more suffering and self-denial than simply giving up chocolate for Lent. It demands nothing less than a constant dying to self."[23]

Scott Hahn

4. Saint Paul explains the condition of the baptized Christian in Romans 8:12-18.

a. What does it mean to live "according to the flesh"? What happens to us if we live "according to the flesh"?

_____

_____

_____

b. How are those who are "led by the Spirit" to live?

_____

_____

_____

c. What is the "spirit of slavery"? What is the "spirit of sonship"? What is the important distinction made between the two?

_____

_____

_____

_____

_____

[23] Scott Hahn, *A Father Who Keeps His Promises* (Ann Arbor, MI: Servant Publications, 1998), 18.

d. What must we do in order to be considered fellow heirs with Christ? What do you think this has to do with discipline?

_____

_____

_____

_____

5. The purpose of a disciplined life is to thwart the temptations of the devil and become all we were intended to be. We know how to live a disciplined life because Jesus has gone before us and has inspired the authors of the Gospels to tell us about His life. Read Matthew 4:1-11, which discusses Jesus' temptation in the desert.

How did Jesus prepare Himself for the temptation of the devil?

_____

_____

_____

Why do you think He chose this means of preparation?

_____

_____

_____

How should we discipline ourselves and prepare ourselves for temptation?

_____

_____

_____

_____

6. Through Jesus' actions and words, He taught us how we are to live. In Matthew 6:1-20, He lays out the three essential disciplines of the Christian way of life: almsgiving, prayer, and fasting. Read Matthew 6:1-20 and complete the following chart.

	How?	Benefit?
Almsgiving		
Prayer		
Fasting		

How do these forms of discipline help us to reform and conform to God's plan for our deeds, words, and minds? Why do you think these are the three essential Christian disciplines?

_____

_____

_____

"To put it simply, God is urging us to make our actions consistent with the demands of our faith. For our sanctity, the holiness we should be striving for is not a second-class sanctity. . . . So I say to you, if you want to become a thorough-going Christian— and I know you are willing, even though you often find it difficult to conquer yourself or to keep climbing upwards with this poor body of ours—then you will have to be very attentive to the minutest of details, for the holiness that our Lord demands of you is to be achieved by carrying out with love of God your work and your daily duties, and these will almost always consist of small realities."[24]

Blessed Josemaría Escrivá

7. According the following passages, describe some characteristics and consequences of an undisciplined life.

a. Proverbs 5:21-23

b. Proverbs 25:28

c. Psalm 50:16-23

8. Based on what Scripture has to say regarding the undisciplined life, reflect upon your life and discern how you have been disciplined and in what ways you need to improve.

How can you incorporate the disciplines of almsgiving, prayer, and fasting into your life? How will this help you to be the person you were made to be?

_____

_____

_____

9. Holiness can only be attained through a deliberate choice to cooperate with God's grace. We must choose to order our lives, to prioritize in conformity with God's plan for us. Reflect upon your daily life. Take some time to look over your planner. Do your days reflect your pursuit of holiness? Take some time now

---

[24] Bl. Josemaría Escrivá, *Friends of God* (Princeton, NJ: Scepter Publishers, 1977), 7-8.

to modify or rework your schedule to prioritize your spiritual life. Things you will want to consider putting in your schedule include daily Mass, frequent—perhaps even weekly—Confession, daily prayer time, and daily Bible and spiritual reading. Use Appendix II.

_____

_____

_____

10. The Church has given us a liturgical year with seasons and days of penance and discipline. In what details of life can you practice small acts of discipline (or penance) in addition to these "Church-mandated" practices? Some suggestions include giving up one small thing every meal (i.e., salt), wearing simple clothing, smiling when you don't want to, etc.

_____

_____

_____

"The way of perfection passes by way of the Cross. There is no holiness without renunciation and spiritual battle. Spiritual progress entails the ascesis and mortification that gradually lead to living in the peace and joy of the Beatitudes."

Catechism, no. 2015

Memory Verse
"Therefore gird up your minds, be sober,
set your hope fully upon the grace that is coming to you
at the revelation of Jesus Christ."
1 Peter 1:13

APPENDIX I:
SUGGESTIONS FOR QUIET TIMES WITH GOD

1. Make an appointment with God every day. Write it in your planner and keep it as you would keep any other appointment. It is important to remember, however, that prayer should not be limited to a time slot, so try to remain recollected throughout your day. Remember to "pray constantly" (1 Thess. 5:17).

2. Find a quiet place, preferably before the Blessed Sacrament. However, Jesus wants to spend time with us anytime and anywhere. If a church is not accessible, enjoy some peaceful time with God in another place.

3. Jesus loves us and wants us to have a conversation with Him. Simply conversing with God, offering Him our hearts, worship, and concerns, pleases Him and helps us to know Him and ourselves better.

4. Keep a prayer journal. Write your prayer intentions, feelings, troubles, worship, verses you want to remember, etc.—the possibilities are endless. A prayer journal is helpful for times when you are having trouble concentrating, and it is a great way of reflecting on what God has accomplished in your life.

5. A possible format for your quiet time is the **ACTS** method of prayer: **A**doration (praise), **C**ontrition (sorrow for sins), **T**hanksgiving (gratitude), and **S**upplication (intercession).

6. Study a book of the Bible or read sections of a spiritual work. For some recommendations, call Catholics United for the Faith at 1-800-693-2484.

7. The Rosary is essential to a prayer life and a great meditative tool. The next time you pray the Rosary, ask yourself, "Am I praying this Rosary or am I just saying Hail Mary's?" There are many useful pamphlets with meditations on the Rosary that may be found at most Catholic bookstores and gift shops.

8. Ask for the prayers of Our Blessed Mother, your patron saint(s), and guardian angel. When you pray, ask your guardian angel to help you concentrate and protect you from the snares of the devil.

APPENDIX II:
Schedule Planner

	Sunday	Monday	Tuesday	Wednesday	Thursday	Friday	Saturday
4:00 am							
5:00 am							
6:00 am							
7:00 am							
8:00 am							
9:00 am							
10:00 am							
11:00 am							
NOON							
1:00 pm							
2:00 pm							
3:00 pm							
4:00 pm							
5:00 pm							
6:00 pm							
7:00 pm							
8:00 pm							
9:00 pm							
10:00 pm							
11:00 pm							
MIDNIGHT							

LEADER'S GUIDE
GENERAL SUGGESTIONS

Thank you for taking on the task of leading this Bible study. Your willingness to serve God by serving other women is admirable, and He will not forget your good deeds. To help you get started, here are a few general suggestions for leading a small group Bible study.

1. How do you start a Bible study group? Simply ask your friends, colleagues, neighbors, and/or fellow parishioners if they would like to join you in a Bible study. Tell them what the study is about and when and where you would like to meet. It is helpful if you are able to meet at an agreed-upon time and place, preferably once a week and in someone's home. Because this Bible study is designed to facilitate discussion, a small number of members is preferable. A group of five or six is ideal, but a few less or more would be fine.

2. You should cover approximately one chapter a week in 1-2 hours. However, some chapters may take more time depending on the amount of group discussion. It is okay if a chapter takes more than one week to cover.

3. The atmosphere of the Bible study should be comfortable and non-threatening. It is important that everyone feels respected and is able to share her thoughts. You may want to provide refreshments or have group members take turns providing a small treat.

4. Each meeting time should begin and end with prayer. It is also a good idea to have members share their personal prayer requests and make a commitment to pray for one another throughout the week.

5. As leader, your job will be to facilitate and move along the discussion, as well as to correct any misunderstandings. You will want to prepare for the Bible study by doing the assigned chapter and preparing extra questions you will ask. The other members should prepare for the study time by completing the assigned chapter before they arrive.

6. Spend some time each week praying for the success of the Bible study and each of the women in your group.

Answers, Information, and More Questions

The second part of the Leader's Guide contains the answers to the objective questions, additional background information, and questions for group discussion. The answers to the questions are marked with an "A," suggested questions for discussion are denoted by "Q" and printed in italics, and "I" sets off any additional information. You may feel free to include or leave out any of the questions and information in your weekly study.

Lesson 1
Holiness 101

1-2. Give the women opportunity to share their ideas. These questions will help to acquaint those who do not know one another and deepen friendships among those who are already friends.

3. A: Everyone.
I: 1 Peter 1:16 quotes Leviticus 11:44.

4. A: The Pharisees were so concerned with following the letter of the law and exterior faithfulness that they neglected the interior life and the more important matters: justice, mercy, and faith (Mt. 23:23).
I: The Pharisees were self-appointed guardians of Israel's faith and were concerned with ritual purity and maintaining the letter of the Law. The Sadducees were conservative, priestly aristocrats, centered in Jerusalem, and the appointed official leaders of Israel.

Q: *What causes Christians to be intimidated by holiness? What could be the cause of Christians' misunderstanding of holiness? What were some of your misunderstandings?*

5. A:
a. Keep the commandments.
b. Do not commit adultery, do not steal, do not bear false witness, honor your father and mother, love your neighbor as yourself.
c. Sell his possessions and give to the poor and he would have treasures in heaven.
d. Treasures in heaven. The young man was righteous in terms of obeying the law but he did not love God more

than himself. He had simply done the bare minimum, but nothing beyond, which would have merited him rewards in heaven. The young man lacked love.

e. Jesus was asking the young man to love God more than himself—to show God that He was more important to him than the riches and things of this life. This was difficult because the young man lacked the love required to do what Jesus asked.

f. Share answers as a group.

6. A:

a. Set our hearts right, be steadfast and prudent, and accept hardships.

b. Detachment from the world.

c. Humility, prayer, repentance.

d. Hunger and thirst for righteousness.

e. Keep alert and be sober. Apply truths to life: Make an act of the will, live simply, ask for someone to keep us accountable to our resolutions.

Q: *How do we prepare ourselves for temptations and trials? How can we be detached from the world? What is humility? How can we, in practical ways, "thirst" for righteousness?*

7. A:

a. God loves us unconditionally. When we were most unlovable, He sent His Son to die for our sins.

b. Merciful, saved us while we were sinners, and gave us the honor of sitting with His Son in heaven.

c. God loved us and died for us while we were still sinners.

d. God will one day enable us to worship Him before His throne.

8. A:
a. Putting riches and things of the world before God.
b. The devil.
c. Love of the world.

Causes: upbringing, culture, disordered passions, the Fall, etc.;

Battles: disordered love, materialism, selfishness, etc.;

Combat: discipline, frequent Mass, Confession, prayer, etc.

9. A:

Soil	Response	Result	Jesus' Explanation
1. the path	1. never took root	1. birds devoured it	1. Satan takes away the Word
2. rocky ground	2. seed sprung up immediately	2. no root so sun scorched it	2. souls start strong but fall away because of persecution
3. among thorns	3. yielded nothing	3. thorns grew up and choked it	3. unfruitful because riches and worldly cares stifle it
4. good soil	4. yielded grain	4. 30-60-100-fold harvest	4. souls who hear and accept the Word and bear fruit

Rocky Soil: allow the Word to take root through prayer and study and prepare ourselves for tribulations.

Thorny Soil: through prayer and discipline, live simply and avoid the cares of the world.

10. Allow some time for the women to share their experiences of the first chapter of this Bible study.

11. Ask the women to share their goals for the week and how they will practically meet them.

MEMORY VERSE: You may want to print out the memory verse on note cards or pretty paper and give them to the women to help them memorize the verse for the following meeting time. You could agree to say it together at the next meeting time.

Lesson 2
The Dignity of Womanhood

1-3. Share your ideas as a group.

4. A:
   a. To till and keep it; "You may freely eat of every tree of the garden; but of the tree of the knowledge of good and evil you shall not eat"; die.
   b. "But for man there was not found a helper fit for him"; woman is to be man's helper. Allow the women to share their thoughts.
   c. From the rib of Adam; because she is "bone of my bones and flesh of my flesh . . . she was taken out of Man"; ecstatic—"This at last . . ."
   d. She was taken out of man and they are two "pieces of a puzzle" that belong back together again. The woman is needed as his helpmate and companion.

I: The woman could be called the "crown of creation" because things were still incomplete without the creation of woman.

5. A:
   a. He was nearby.
   b. Adam must have told her.
   c. He tempted her with pride.
   d. Eve gave it to him.
   e. Adam first, Eve second, and the serpent was addressed last but without a question from God who simply gave him his due curse. Adam's job was to "till and keep" the garden. The words to "till and keep" literally refer to Adam's responsibility to cultivate and guard the garden and its contents. He shirked his responsibility to guard

his wife by allowing the serpent, a malicious intruder, to interrogate his wife and allure her to sin. Adam was more responsible for their failure and so God addressed him first.

Q: *Did Adam fulfill his duties? How is Adam's failure played out in the concupiscence of men today?*

 f. Adam blamed the woman and the woman blamed the serpent.

Q: *How does this reflect the all too often response of a person caught in wrongdoing?*

 g. Serpent: God crushed Satan the prideful tempter, bringing him physically low—so low he now crawls on his stomach and eats the dust of the ground. The announcement of his ultimate demise was also proclaimed by the crushing of his head by the woman and her seed (i.e., Mary and Jesus, Gen. 3:15). Woman: pain in childbirth and subject to the excesses of male domination. Man: his productivity will only come with sweat and hard labor and his body (and woman's) are now subject to death and bodily corruption.

 h. God had a plan from the beginning to redeem the world, and He didn't want us to destroy our hope for redemption by eating of the fruit that would permanently separate us from Him.

I: The preternatural gifts originally given to Adam and Eve were lost to us through their sin. The preternatural gifts are immortality (no physical death), integrity (the body and its senses are properly and easily controlled by the soul), impassibility (no suffering), and infused knowledge. See generally Catechism, nos. 385-421.

6. A: Share opinions and thoughts as a group. A woman's "desire shall be for your husband" and "he shall rule over you" (Gen. 3:16) offer a key to understanding the strife. Many of the pitfalls of the feminist movement involves a reaction to the sin of men and a misunderstanding of the inherent dignity of woman. This is particularly manifested today in the promotion of the masculinization of women. The proper response of men and women needs to be abandonment to the grace of God given us in the New Covenant and, through that grace, the restoration of our original dignity, integrity, and harmony. See also Catechism, nos. 1606-08.

7. A:
  a. In the midst of a large crowd, Jesus told this woman that her faith had healed her and set her faith as an example for others.
  b. He used this poor widow as a model of good behavior.
  c. Jesus spoke with an adulterous Samaritan woman and revealed to her the truths of His Kingdom and told her of the Messiah. In this scene, Jesus taught His disciples that He came to save even Samaritans and sinners, and that a woman could be entrusted with the important truths of God.
  d. He forgave the woman caught in adultery and showed her mercy when others were not willing to do so.

Jesus' culture often abused and disrespected women. Jesus treated women with dignity and respect.

I: The Samaritan people were Israelites who intermarried with foreigners after the Assyrians devastated northern Palestine in 722 B.C. (see 2 Kings 17). They were no longer pure Israelites in the eyes of the Jews and were often branded as "Gentiles" and "sinners" who distorted Jewish beliefs and no longer worshipped in the Jerusalem Temple. This longstanding conflict between Jews and Samaritans makes Jesus' conversation with the woman of Samaria and his parable of the Good Samaritan stand out in contrast to the thought of His day. He thus used this conflict as a "teachable moment" to promote His purpose of bringing peace to the people of earth.

8. A:
   a. Many women. Mary Magdalene, Mary the mother of James and Joseph, and the mother of the sons of Zebedee (James and John).
   b. Mary Magdalene, Mary the mother of James and Joses, Salome, and many other women.
   c. Women followers from Galilee.
   d. Mary, Jesus' mother, Mary's sister, Mary, wife of Clopas, and Mary Magdalene, the apostle John.

   John was the only apostle of Jesus at the crucifixion.

   The God-given gift of women to love courageously is shown clearly in these Gospel accounts.

9. A:
   a. Mary Magdalene.
   b. Mary Magdalene.

Jesus again raised the dignity of women as he made Mary Magdalene according to Pope John Paul II in *Mulieris Dignitatem*, no. 16, "The apostle of the Apostles."

   I. Mary loved Jesus desperately and devotedly. This saint was a great sinner until Jesus healed her of her demonic possession and she reformed her life. She stood faithfully at the foot of the Cross and she, along with other women from Galilee, had gone to prepare the body of Jesus for proper burial.

Lesson 3
Faith and the Life of Grace

1. A:

How is faith acquired? Philippians 1:29	"granted to you . . . believe in Him"—it is only through the grace of God that we are able to believe. Faith is a gift from God.
What is faith? Hebrews 11:1	"assurance of things hoped for" and "conviction of things not seen"
What is faith's importance? Hebrews 11:6	"without faith it is impossible to please" God

2. A: "things hoped for": forgiveness of sins and salvation through the merits of Jesus on the Cross; "things not seen": the crucifixion and resurrection of Jesus Christ and His reign in Heaven.

3. A:

Person(s)	Deed(s)
Abel	offered an acceptable sacrifice; approved as righteous by God
Enoch	his faith pleased God and he was rewarded by being spared death
Noah	built an ark even though he had never seen rain
Abraham	called by God, went out into the Land of Promise, not knowing where he was going; offered his son Isaac as he believed God could raise men from the dead

Sarah	conceived a child in old age because she believed God would accomplish what He had promised
Isaac	blessed Jacob and Esau
Jacob	blessed the sons of Joseph
Joseph	spoke of the exodus and gave directions for his burial
Moses	accepted abuse rather than be associated with sin, left Egypt, kept the Passover
The People	crossed the Red Sea, the walls of Jericho fell
Rahab	welcomed spies and did not die
Gideon, Barak, Samson, Jephthah, David, Samuel, and the prophets	conquered all kinds of evils and spoke of the promises of God
Women and others	the dead were raised, martyred

4. A:
  a. We must have both faith and do God's will.
  b. If we believe and obey we will have eternal life.
  c. The ministry of the disciples of Jesus is to "bring about the obedience of faith."
  d. It is not obedience for its own sake that is advantageous, but rather obedience or "working love" resulting from faith.

5. A:

	Mt. 15:21-28	Mk. 5:24-34	Lk. 1:26-38
What was her faith in?	the power of Jesus to heal	the power of Jesus to heal	the power of God to accomplish the impossible
How did she show her faith?	she persistently called after Jesus and called Him "master"	she touched His robe believing that this would heal her	she believed the words of the angel and accepted and believed the miracle to be done to her by God
What was God's response to her faith?	He proclaimed that she had great faith and answered her request	He told her that her faith had healed her	He made her the Mother of God and the most blessed among creatures
How was her life different because of her faith?	her daughter was healed of the demonic possession	she was healed of her illness	she was the Mother of God and became the "Queen of Heaven"

Q: *How does the faith of these women inspire you to greater faith?*

6. A: Share as a group the responses.

7. A:
   a. His flesh and blood.
   b. Those who eat it will live forever.
   c. They could not understand how He could give us His flesh and blood to eat and it was opposed to the Jewish regulations forbidding the consumption of blood (Lev. 17:10-14, 19:26; Deut. 12:16, 23-25).
   d. The disciples were having a difficult time understanding how He could give them His body and blood to eat and drink. Jesus asked them if they could not believe this, how

were they going to believe His ascension into heaven? The words that Jesus spoke to them were from the Spirit and required the Spirit to be understood. His words were spirit and life. Their "flesh" (i.e., unaided human reason; see John 8:15), which could not understand His words, was a hindrance to their faith. It is important to note that Jesus was not referring to His flesh, for He had just said that His flesh would be a source of life to the world, but rather "the flesh" here refers to the weakness of human nature in general.

Q: *Does your reading of John 6:47-63 inspire you to receive the Holy Eucharist often? What does the institution of the Blessed Sacrament teach us about Jesus' love for us?*

8. A: As St. Paul says, we need to examine ourselves and be sure that we are receiving the Body of Our Lord in a worthy manner, which means not bringing the holy Jesus into a soul that is separated from Him through mortal sin. (See Catechism, nos. 1385, 1854-64.) It is the highest earthly privilege to receive the Body of Christ so that we can become like Him. If we receive Jesus unworthily, we are profaning His body, or making a mockery of that which is sacred and bringing condemnation upon ourselves.

9. A: The Eucharist helps us to become holy by allowing us to receive the Holy One within our very being. We receive all that Jesus is when we receive Communion, meaning that we receive His body, blood, soul, and divinity so that we can become more like Him.

Lesson 4
To Serve Is to Reign!

1. A:
a. Everlasting love, continued faithfulness out of love.
b. God loves us as He loves Jesus.
c. While we were sinners, God loved us and died to save us.
d. We are children of God and not slaves.

Share adjectives.

God loves us first, faithfully, and to death.

2. Share ideas and experiences as a group. It is important to remember that we are children of God and not slaves. As children of a Great King we should behave and love with the same dignity and love given us.

3. A:
a. Tongues, prophecy, knowledge of mysteries, faith, alms-giving, martyrdom—all of these are nothing without love.
b. Patient, kind, not jealous, does not brag, not arrogant, does not act shamefully or seek its own interests, is not easily angered or think about wrongs done against it, is not happy with sin but with truth, love suffers, believes, hopes and endures all things and never fails.

Q: *These characteristics of love have become almost a cliché in our society. Why? What does it take to live out this definition of love? How does knowing that God loves you like this inspire you to return His love?*

c. Love supersedes them all.
d. Speak, think, and reason as a child.
e and f. Share as a group.

4. A:

    a. A good person will do good deeds. If he does not, he will not inherit the kingdom of God—simply proclaiming Jesus as Lord is not enough.

    b. Faith manifesting itself through works done out of love is the heart of the Christian faith.

    c. Abraham was justified by his works only when he offered them as an act of faith.

5. A:

    a. Fear, love, serve, and obey God.

    b. Love is the fulfillment of the Law and so we are to love our neighbor as ourselves.

    c. Lay down our lives for our neighbors.

6. A:

    a. God's will became her will and she was willing to serve God no matter the cost.

    b. Share responses as a group.

    c. Mary accepted whatever God asked of her. She gave Him an unconditional "yes" to all He had planned for her life.

    d. Love=Service: Holiness is saying "yes" to God all the time. It is a complete submission to the will of God no matter the cost.

7. A:

    a. If you want to be holy, you must be a servant as He is a servant of all.

    b. Through being a servant, or being last, we shall be first in the kingdom of God.

8. A: Share your ideas and resolutions as a group.

Lesson 5
Prayer: The Way to a New Heart

1. A: Encourage the women to share their ideas and experiences. Emphasize that it is never too late to change our habits.

2. A:
   a. God desires to answer our prayers if only we would ask.
   b. Prayer is a powerful tool to help us avoid temptation and God desires us to be on our guard.
   c. We are to persevere in praying in the Spirit continuously for fellow Christians.
   d. Pray all the time.
   e. Be faithful and constant in prayer.

God communicates throughout these verses that prayer is our weapon against temptation and the tricks of the devil because it keeps us in touch with Him who is our strength. God desires us to be close to Him, and prayer is the primary way to foster that relationship. We can more faithfully obey God's commands to be steadfast in prayer by being disciplined about our prayer life. Committing yourself to a specific prayer time and writing it in your planner is one easy way to make prayer a priority. Brainstorm about other ideas as a group.

3. A:
   a. If we are in God's will, whatever we ask of Him will be done for us.
   b. We will find the Lord if we seek after Him with our whole heart and soul.

c. Believe in the power of prayer and God's willingness to answer and we will receive what we have asked for.

d. God promises to be near to those who pray to Him and give those who fear Him what they desire.

e. The prayers of a righteous person are very powerful and can accomplish much.

4. A:

	Luke 11:5-13	Luke 18:1-8	Luke 18:9-14
How are we to pray?	consistently, persistently	consistently, persistently	humbly
What is the result of prayer?	get our heart's desire	God will not delay in answering us, and we will be vindicated	justification
How can you apply this teaching?			

5. A:

1. exaltation and worship of God;
2. request for God's kingdom and will to reign on earth;
3. request for our physical needs; and
4. request for forgiveness and spiritual needs.

Q: *What would the world look like if His will were done here on earth?*

6. A:

	Jesus' Prayer Life
When?	morning, all night
How?	three times He made the same request; conversationally spoke to God the Father
Where?	lonely place; on a mountain; wilderness; Gethsemane
What?	God's will be done; for Christians: protection from evil; unity; our sanctification and eternal salvation

7. A: Hannah humbly, fervently, and tearfully prayed for a son. After she prayed, she was peaceful and resigned to the will of God. After God gave Hannah the son she desired, she responded with thanksgiving and was a good steward of His blessing.

I: It is important to note that children are always considered a blessing from God. See Ps. 127:3-5, and 128:3-4; see generally Catechism, nos. 2373-79.

8. A: Share responses as a group. Encourage the women to keep one another accountable by asking one another how well they are keeping their commitments.

Lesson 6
Obedience: The Proof of Our Love

1. A:
   a. If we do the will of God in our lives, we will be saved.
   b. If we live according to the rules of the Christian life, we will receive our prize: heaven.
   c. Those who are disobedient will not attain eternal life.
   d. If we do the will of God, we will live forever in heaven.

These verses all highlight the justice of God.

2. A:
   a. If we love Him, we will obey His commandments.
   b. Obedience is proof of loving God.
   c. Love for God is obedience.
   d. We are considered God's friends if we obey.

The privilege of loving God through obedience is being called His friend.

   Q: *Have you ever thought or realized that obedience=love for God? What does obedient love "look like" practically? What does it mean to be someone's friend? What are the privileges of friendship? What are the privileges and responsibilities of being God's friend?*

3. A:
   a. Fruit of deeds will be good.
   b. Live in God's love, joy.
   c. Actions blessed by God.

4. A:

a. We will receive rewards for the good we have done.

b. Receive a crown of glory.

c. God will repay us according to what we have done.

d. We will again have the right to the tree of life (see Gen. 3).

I: For a better understanding of the last things, please refer to Catechism, nos. 1010-50. You may choose to read and discuss this section as a group.

5. A:

a. God will provide a way to escape the temptation.

b. Change our desire.

c. Do not grow weary and resist sin to the point of martyrdom.

Q: *How do these verses encourage you to fight the battle against sin?*

6. A: Sapphira was the wife of Ananias.

She did not honor a commitment to give proceeds of the sale of property to the Church.

She lied to hide her sin and was struck dead.

Peter told Sapphira that she and her husband tempted the Spirit and lied to God.

When we sin, we sin against God.

7. A:

   a. Satan and his demons.

   b. The sword of the Spirit (the Word of God) and prayer.

   c. The Word of God and prayer weaken the devil and strengthen the soul to be obedient.

   d. Share responses. <u>Suggestions</u>: memorize Scripture, daily prayer times, Rosary.

8. Share responses as a group.

Lesson 7
Purity: The Way to See God

1-2. Share answers as a group.

3. A:
   a. Because we are children of God.
   b. We will be useful and ready to do good works.
   c. We will be near to God and He will come near to us.

4. A:
   a. Ability to "see God."
   b. Answered prayers.
   c. Eternal life.
   d. God is good to us.

5. This statement can be understood as seeing God in heaven as well as knowing the truths of God here on earth.

6. A:
   a. Have no idols, do not live a lie; or positively, live a life of integrity.
   b. Guard your heart.
   c. "Put to death" sinful, worldly actions and habits.
   d. Put all hope in God.

   Q: *What does it mean to live a life of integrity? How do you guard your heart? How do you put all your hope in God?*

7. A: Modesty involves guarding your own senses and guarding others against sin.

8. A:
   a. Modestly, discreetly, not too costly.
   b. Simply.
   c. Modestly.
   d. The fear of the Lord is the source of beauty for women.

These verses describe the behavior of a woman who desires to be godly and reverent. Her actions are done with a gentle, quiet spirit. These principles apply to single women and girls as well as to married women.

9. Discuss the interconnectedness of the Body of Christ, the Christian faithful, and our responsibility to build up one another in virtue and holiness. It is important to emphasize that Christian men and women are responsible to protect each other from falling into temptation or sin.

10. Clothing that does not draw too much attention to the wearer or lead another to sin. Long dresses and loose-fitting attire should be "safe." You may want to discuss that dressing modestly does not necessarily mean being unfashionable. It means choosing fashions that maintain and protect your dignity as a virtuous Christian woman.

11. Share your ideas as a group.

Lesson 8
Discipline: The Practice of the Christian Life

1. Share ideas as a group.

2. A:
   a. St. Paul laments that even he struggles to control his deeds even though his mind has been conformed to law of God.
   b. The tongue is able to do the most damage and is the most difficult part of our bodies to control.
   c. We need to become holy, and the first step toward making our bodies holy is transforming our minds to discern the will of God.

   Q: *Which area do you struggle in the most: thoughts, words, or deeds? Why does it become easier to obey God if we reform our minds? Why do you think St. Paul says that even with a renewed mind it is difficult to control the body?*

3. A: A disciplined life is the way to eternal life.

4. A:
   a. If a Christian chooses to "live according to the flesh," she is a slave to her bodily passions and desires and will die, i.e., or not live in God's grace and receive eternal life.
   b. Those who are "led by the Spirit" live as children of God and not as slaves to sin.
   c. The "spirit of slavery" means being bound and controlled by our own bodily desires, living without faith or love. The "spirit of sonship" is living as a child of the King of the Universe, free from bodily passions—a life obedient to our Father. A child of God must live "by the Spirit" in order to overcome slavery to the flesh and live in the freedom of Christ and be His heir.

d. In order to be considered a fellow heir of Christ, we must suffer with Him.

5. A: Jesus fasted forty days and nights.

I: Fasting is an ancient practice of many religions, especially Christianity. Fasting is a powerful way of laying aside the desires of the body for the good of the soul. A person who wants to fast might consider choosing a particular day or two of the week, traditionally Wednesday and Friday. It is important to note here that although we are no longer bound to the specific penance of abstinence from meat on Friday (except during Lent), the Church continues to require us to do some form of penance on each Friday of the year. See Catechism, nos. 1434-39, 2043.

6. A:

	How?	Benefit?
Almsgiving	give discreetly	God will reward you; teaches generosity, simplicity, and sacrifice
Prayer	pray discreetly, humbly	God will reward you; teaches humility, discipline, and sacrifice
Fasting	fast secretly, try to look your best so others will not notice that you are fasting	God will reward you; teaches the body to submit to the will

These disciplines teach us to put our spiritual needs above our bodily needs and desires. Then we can become truly free.

7. A:
a. A sinful man will become enslaved to his sin and he will die.
b. An undisciplined life is useless.
c. The wicked and undisciplined God will disown, while the disciplined will be saved.

8-10. Discuss as a group and share your ideas.

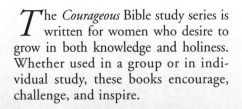